SEQUOIA

Sequoia Patterson

Dedication

To every reader standing in the soil of their own survival—may you see in these pages what the sequoia tree knows: that from buried roots, greatness grows.

Acknowledgements

First and foremost, to **my husband and my children** — you all are my heart, my reason, and my greatest accomplishment. Everything I do, I do with you all in mind. Thank you all for your patience, your love, and for believing in me even when I didn't believe in myself. You all are the light that keeps me grounded and the fire that keeps me going. Every page in this book carries pieces of your love and strength.

To my **family and friends**, thank you for standing by me through every season — through the laughter, the tears, the long nights, and the quiet moments of doubt. You reminded me who I was when I started to forget. Your words, prayers, and presence gave me courage when I needed it most. I love you all deeply and am forever grateful for the way you've held me down with love and faith.

To **Julie Taylor**, thank you for introducing me to the **College and Community Fellowship (CCF)** organization. That introduction changed my life. Through CCF, I found not only professional growth, but a sense of purpose and community that pushed me to rise higher and dream bigger.

To **Dr. Nadia Lopez** and the entire **College and Community Fellowship** family, thank you for seeing something in me that I hadn't yet seen in myself. You believed in my story, in my strength, and in my voice — and because of that, I am now a **published best-selling author**. You helped me step into my calling, and for that, I am forever grateful.

To **Sheryl Prince** and **Noire Publishing House**, your coaching, guidance, and love helped me bring this dream to life. You reminded me that my story mattered and that my words could heal. Thank you for walking beside me, for every conversation, every push, and every moment of encouragement that helped me bring this book into the world.

Preface

There comes a time in life when you stop asking to be seen—and start showing up as yourself. That's what this book is about. It's me, Sequoia—not the version the world expects, but the woman who has learned to grow through every storm.

I've lived many lives inside this one. I've been the girl who didn't know her worth, the woman who gave too much, and the mother who had to keep going no matter how tired she was. I've been silent when I should've screamed, and strong when I wanted to fall apart. Every version of me had a story—and all of them deserve to be told.

This book isn't about perfection or pity. It's about truth—the kind that sits heavy until you finally let it out. My truth comes with pain and peace, love and loss, heartbreak and healing. It's all part of who I am.

Sequoia isn't just my name. It's a reminder that even when life tries to cut me down, my roots still remember how to rise. It's about growth that doesn't need permission. About learning to stand tall—not because life was easy, but because I refused to stay buried.

If you're holding this book, I hope you see pieces of yourself in these pages. I hope you remember that your story has power and that even the broken parts can bloom again.

This is me, finally standing in my truth.

This is *Sequoia*.

From my heart to yours—thank you for believing in me.

— *Sequoia Patterson*

TABLE OF CONTENTS

Chapter 1

The Birth of the Storm

The sun—no matter the weather—is always going to shine. That's what I think about when the storm comes my way.

But my storms? They're different. They start out rough and end just as rough. I hate the pressure. And most of all, I hate the storm itself.

I try to understand why I'm always caught in these storms—like no one else is supposed to feel this pain except me?! Am I the only one meant to endure the storm? Like, how the hell does the storm always know where to find me?

And when I tell people I've been in the storm, they brush it off. I wonder if people even know the pain of a storm and how bad it affects me. Those that do know it, think because they survived, I'll survive too. But if that's true, why wouldn't they tell me about the dangers? Why not warn me and tell me what to watch out for?

My first storm came when I was six or seven—that's as far back as I can remember.

One weekend, my mom was cleaning out her bedroom closet when my cousin came to visit. Family visiting wasn't unusual. My family was close-knit, at least that's the word people used to describe us. And me, being my mom's only child, I guess they loved seeing me when they came over.

While my mother cleaned her closet, my cousin and I chilled in the living room. He told me to sit on his lap and did this little bouncy thing he does with his knee. There I was, legs spread wide open across his. I thought it was just to keep me steady, so I sat and enjoyed the ride as usual.

Most times, after the "fun" ride came a kiss and a pat on the butt. My mom called him into the bedroom briefly. While they talked, I went to lay in the bed under the covers.

It's like I knew exactly what to do. After my mom and cousin talked, me and my cousin "played." Under the sheets, his hands always landed in the same place—right between my legs. It was a strange feeling. Like the pulsing from the ride was still there. The more his hands moved, the more it felt good. I guess I wasn't sure what the feeling was. This was the "Quiet Storm".

The smell of pine, bleach, bacon, and eggs—with a hint of marijuana—seeped into my dreams. It was Sunday. Momma never missed a chance to clean while I was sleeping. She'd wake me by wiping me down with rubbing alcohol, muttering something like, "I gotta get the devil off of her.

Now that I'm older, I wonder if the devil and the "quiet" storm are the same for me and my mom—just different names. I wonder if she knew and just didn't care. Or maybe she felt there was nothing she could do about it. Perhaps she was scared to face the storm. I'm not sure either way.

As my eyes opened, I saw my mother—slim mocha-brown skin, an Afro the size of Wakanda, one long beaded braid hanging to the side. She smiled, her natural white teeth gleaming. "Good morning, Candy," she said. That was the name my dad gave me. I'm not sure why, especially since I wasn't even allowed to eat candy.

"Breakfast is done. Go brush your teeth and wash your face."

To get to the bathroom, I had to pass my mom's bed. We lived in a big one-bedroom apartment divided into two halves—her side and mine. As I passed her bed, I saw my dad lying there. "Good morning, baby girl. How was your sleep?" He asked. "It was good," I said.

After brushing my teeth, I headed to the table for breakfast. At the table, my parents started arguing—about my dad's cheating. I don't think my mother really cared that he cheated. She was more concerned about who he cheated with. Their voices got louder as tensions rose.

I interrupted. "Mom, can I have some juice?" just to stop them from getting physical.

She got up and went to the kitchen. My dad leaned over and kissed me on the forehead. "I'll see you later," he said—not even halfway through breakfast. But I knew that he wasn't coming back later as promised.

After their fights, he'd disappear for weeks. And when he returned, it was with coloring books and teddy bears for me, hugs and kisses for my mother. I guess that was his way of apologizing.

They'd go into the room and close the door. At my young age, I shouldn't have known what was going on in there, but I did. 'Cause every time the storm came for me, the door was closed, too.

The only difference between me and Momma when it came to storms? She smiled when hers was over.

Reader Reflection

Take a moment to pause. Breathe. You've just stepped through my storm—now it's time to reflect on your own.

Use this space to write or simply to settle your thoughts. There's no right or wrong here—only truth.

What does "the storm" mean to you?

_____

_____

_____

_____

_____

_____

The sun—no matter the weather—is always going to shine. How does that line make you feel?

_____

_____

_____

_____

_____

_____

Who taught you how to survive your storms?

_____

_____

_____

_____

_____

_____

What emotions surfaced for you while reading this chapter?

_____

_____

_____

_____

_____

_____

What do you need to release before turning the page?

_____

_____

_____

_____

_____

_____

Remember: Even the fiercest storm eventually runs out of rain. Let this page hold what your heart is ready to let go of.

Chapter 2

Not Crazy, Just Unseen

Monday morning rolled around and it was time for school. School wasn't far—just down the block and I actually loved going. The memories that stuck with me started around fourth grade, when the storms began to shift and my behavior followed the same path of chaos.

I had this fat ass white teacher who couldn't stand me. She always had her face screwed up like she smelled shit. Every little thing I did, she was on the phone with my mother.

The last time she called was Halloween. We were allowed to wear costumes, but my mom was a Jehovah's Witness, so that meant no holidays, no costumes, and no trick-or-treating. But this year, I decided I was celebrating Halloween.

At first, I wanted to go as a ghost. But knowing my mother, she'd look at a sheet and swear it was a KKK outfit. Then I remembered my godmother bought me two skirts—one silver, one black. That's when I had the idea—I'd go as a prostitute. I don't know where that thought came from. Maybe the idea of having control over how men viewed me was the motivation.

I grabbed a pair of my mom's fishnet stockings, slipped some Skippies on my feet, and went through her dresser for makeup and lipstick. That was my costume. Of course, I knew Momma wasn't about to let me walk out the house like that, so I smuggled the outfit to school and changed in the bathroom.

Standing in front of that cracked mirror, fishnets up to my knees, cheap lipstick smeared across my mouth—I felt powerful. This was the version of me that nobody could control. Not my mom, not my teacher, nor the kids who teased me.

At that moment, I wasn't thinking about the consequences. I thought about how heads would turn and all the attention I'd get. Maybe I wanted to prove that I could be whoever I decided to be. Or perhaps I just wanted to feel grown for the day. Whatever it was, I reveled in it. Besides, I looked good as hell. But of course, my teacher didn't agree and called my mom.

When I heard that she was on her way, I ran to the bathroom and changed back into my regular clothes. But not before I took one last look in the mirror. *Damn,* I thought. *This outfit is fucking original. Nobody else has this and I didn't even spend a dime.* Still, if I didn't want my ass beat, I needed to get out of it quick.

My mom being called out of work was never a good thing. As I sat in the principal's office, all I could think was, "These motherfuckers are in there telling her all types of shit, because none of them like me anyway." The door opened. Everyone was smiling—except my mother.

On the walk home, she started her lecture about how important school was, how lucky I was that they didn't call BCW. Her words

8

blurred out, fading into the background. I was too busy plotting how to avoid the beating I knew was coming.

If I went into the bedroom and started cleaning, I might get trapped because of the way the beds were set up. If I went to the kitchen to do the dishes, that was risky because the kitchen was the smallest room in the house so there was room to escape.

By the time we reached the door, my mother's voice was rising. I made a quick dash to the bathroom. If she wanted to beat me, she was going to have to wait. Sitting there on the toilet, heart pounding, I thought about the last time the school had called BCW.

I was an only child, so of course I had imaginary friends. But mine weren't just friends—they were my siblings. I used to sit in the closet across from the one with all the garbage bags of clothes and play with my imaginary brother and sister. Every day after homework, I'd crawl in there, feed them scraps and talk to them like they were real. The funny thing was, every time I came back, the food was gone.

One day, that same fat ass teacher asked me if I had siblings. I said, "Yeah—one brother, one sister."

"Do they go to this school?" she asked.

"No," I said. "They live in the closet. My mom doesn't let them out."

Next thing I knew, the school was calling my mom questioning her about these closet kids. She told them they were imaginary. But I was like, *How, Momma? If they're imaginary, why is the food I leave in there always gone?*

Of course, the school called BCW and they came. A man and woman, social workers, came to the house and searched the whole place—opening closets and checking cracks, crevices, and corners. Then, they opened *that* closet and pulled out all of the bags. They found nothing but crumbs and little black droppings. My mother and the social workers laughed, but I didn't get the joke until they explained it. The food wasn't being devoured by my imaginary siblings. Turns out I was feeding mice.

Looking back, I can laugh at the whole BCW mess. But back then, it was serious. I didn't understand why adults never believed me. My siblings weren't real, but the need for them was. And the closet wasn't empty—it was where I built my own safe, little world when the real one felt too unpredictable.

But it wasn't always chaos and confusion with my mom. She had this weird, playful side too—one she only showed when it was just us. Sometimes, she'd pretend we were spies and I was her secret agent. She'd scribble little "mission briefs" on ripped pieces of paper and tuck them under my pillow or slip them into my lunchbox. One day, I remember waking up to a note that said:

Agent 7: Today's mission is critical. Retrieve the goods from the target. Do not break cover. The old man at the liquor store has what we need. Be swift. Be silent. Trust no one.

The "goods" were always the same, her Newports. She'd send me down to the corner liquor store where the old man behind the counter knew her well. He'd hand over the cigarettes without a word, like he was in on the whole thing.

To me, it wasn't about buying cigarettes—it was the mission. Sneaking around, passing notes, and returning with the "package" in hand made me feel important and like I was a part of something. It also made me feel trusted.

Those were the good ole days. My mother knew how to make the smallest things feel like an adventure. Even when life felt like it was falling apart, she had a way of slipping into character. Maybe pretending was her way of escaping. Truth be told, pretending was the only thing that kept me sane.

Reader Reflection

Sometimes we build whole worlds just to be seen in them. Sometimes imagination is the only safe place we have.

This space is for you—to sit with the hidden parts of yourself, the ones that had to pretend, perform, or disappear just to survive.

When in your life did you feel unseen or misunderstood?

_____

_____

_____

_____

_____

What "costume" or disguise have you worn to feel accepted, strong, or safe?

_____

_____

_____

_____

_____

Pretending was the only thing that kept me sane. What does that mean to you?

_____

_____

_____

_____

_____

Were there moments in your childhood when imagination became survival?

_____

_____

_____

_____

_____

What part of your inner child still longs to be believed, protected, or seen?

_____

_____

_____

_____

_____

_____

_____

_____

_____

_____

_____

*Remember: You were never crazy for needing to be seen.
You were simply human—creating light in the dark*

.

Chapter 3

Embers of a Broken Childhood

Over the years, I had become so good at pretending. I don't know if I'd lost touch with reality or if I was just numb. My cousin was still having a field day in my pants, and no one seemed to care to even notice. At some point, oddly enough I became excited to see him. I still don't know if my mother knew what was going on or if she even cared. By this point, it didn't even matter.

She had other fish to fry. Months of my mom and dad arguing—him coming and going—built up until they weren't even together anymore. They became co-parents, nothing more. One day my mom let my dad take me for a week—or maybe it was just a couple of days. Either way, it didn't end well.

My dad thought it was a good idea to book a flight to Virginia. Why? Don't ask me. We slept in some woman's living room—one of his girlfriends—on a bare mattress. No sheets, no blanket—just a raw mattress.

One day, while at this lady's house, my mother called him. Whatever she said, it turned into a crisis. Suddenly, I was a "kidnapped" child. My mother always had a way of turning the world into a five-alarm fire.

The day my father brought me back, all hell broke loose. My mother—five-foot-four and maybe 150 pounds soaking wet—leapt on him and beat that man right in front of his mother's building. She beat him like he was her own son. It was tragic!

I didn't see my father for a long time after that. That fight was my mother's way of finally getting rid of him. He'd return occasionally— never for too long though. But just enough time to stir something in me. Every time he came around, it was always temporary and with a "quick fix". A doll. Some candy. A promise wrapped in a smile. He'd even ask me what I wanted him to bring next time and I'd tell him, believing he'd deliver. But next time never came. Though he promised he'd be right back, I was left waiting and hoping.

My hate for animals started with one of those broken promises. On my birthday, he brought me a little white puppy. I loved that dog instantly—it felt like love from him in a form that wouldn't leave. He said he was going to take the puppy for a walk and come right back. But he never came back. Later I found out that he hadn't been walking *my* dog after all—he'd been walking *her* dog, the woman he cheated on my mother with. I never wanted another dog after that because every bark reminded me of betrayal.

Looking back, I realize that when a father makes promises and doesn't keep them, he leaves behind something heavier than disappointment. He plants a kind of hope that grows wild—hope that someone else will show up the way he didn't. That kind of hope can make a girl chase pieces of men who remind her of the one who first let her down—even when they hurt her, because deep down she's still waiting for someone to keep their word.

With my dad out of the picture, my mom eventually got a new boyfriend. She met him in a record shop in Harlem that he owned. He was tall, handsome, and brown-skinned. Just like my daddy. Good, curly hair and a beard that stood out too. I guess my mother had a type.

After a while of them dating, I noticed my mom changing. She was meaner, angrier, and screamed at me more. Sometimes she even got physical, which had never been her style. Before, her punishments were creative. She'd make me "travel the world" by walking around the block twenty times, or "learn a new language" by writing the same sentence over and over in different ways. But now? Things were different.

The change came with this new thing going around. She was using drugs—not weed. Rock. Crack cocaine. I remember the day I found out. I was sleeping in her bed when I heard a chop-chop sound on a plate. My greedy ass thought I was rolling over to grab some food. But when she realized I was awake, she jumped up and ran out of the room. Don't ask me how I knew it was drugs—I just did. My soul told me.

Later that day, I asked if we could talk. She always let me speak freely, so we sat on the couch in the living room to talk. With the biggest lump in my throat and my chest pounding, I told her, "I don't like your new friend."

She didn't even blink. "Well, I don't like your friends." That was it—conversation over.

Strange, because my mom always let me explain myself before. But not this time or anymore after that.

Months later, she was pregnant with my little sister. I vaguely remember her and that man having a bad fight, so he wasn't around much. I don't even recall him being there after my sister was born.

When my Mom went into labor, I had to stay at a family member's house. That's when the second storm came. And this one was big.

You should be able to trust any adult, right? They are supposed to protect you from harm and keep you safe. Well, it just seems to me like most adult men only know how to cause pain.

The relative my mom left me with went to the store and left my male cousin and me in the house with the "monster". While I was on the couch, playing and flipping around with my cousin, my nightgown slipped and revealed that I wasn't wearing underwear. The monster kept asking me to flip again, so unbeknownst to me, he could prey on me. This wasn't like before—he didn't just use his hands. His mouth gave an extra layer of moisture down there, and when he was satisfied, he instructed me to get on top of him.

That's when I knew my world would never be the same. As I straddled him, the initial pain felt like I was going to die. He then adjusted me how he wanted and gave me specific directions. I was to look out the window and don't stop moving until I saw a red car. That red car never came. Once he had finished his business, he told me to go clean myself up. Not before warning me that if I said anything about what happened that I was going to get in trouble.

This went on the whole time I was there. And I never said anything. Why would I? The first time a man touched me, no one cared. Why would they care now? The only person who knew was my cousin. We carried that ugly secret for years.

After my sister was born, I went back home and became my mom's little helper. She loved to play these "spy kid" games with me. She'd send me to the store on a mission. I had to follow every rule to the

T or the mission would fail. I loved it. It made me feel like a big girl. Besides, now that I had a sister, I wanted more responsibility.

One day, I got my wish. I was given the chance to watch her while my mother went out. She gave me the rules and listed the don'ts. But I wasn't listening because I was too busy imagining the adventure me and my sister were about to go on. Would we slide down waterfalls? Explore caves? Or maybe we'd discover the underworld?

Yes—the underworld. That was it. Nobody I knew had ever been there. Perfect! While my mind wandered, so did my mother's rules. When she asked if I understood, I quickly yelled "Yes!" with so much excitement and glee like I was ready to win a prize. The second she walked out the door, I went into character. We were underworld explorers and had to find the hidden treasure. The only problem? We didn't have any light. The only solution I could think of was the lighter my mother left behind. Fire was light—quick and easy solution.

But how would I keep the light going? That was the challenging part. Then I saw a string hanging from under the bed. Just like that, we had continuous light. The only problem was the light didn't just belong to the underworld. It spread. And before I knew it, my mother's bed was engulfed in flames.

I grabbed my sister, put her on the couch in the living room and ran to the kitchen. The only plan I had was to put the fire out myself. I filled a cake pan with water, rushed back—but by the time I got there, the water was gone. The fire was too much. I had to tell my mother.

Now, don't get me wrong—me being "left in charge" made it sound like she was far away. But the truth was that she was just upstairs. So, I ran up and told her what was going on. She thought I was joking until she saw the smoke. She called the fire department and when they came and put the fire out, one of the firemen turned to her and said, "You should beat her ass."

But my mother had a different idea. She packed me some food, a bag of clothes, handed me a few dollars, and put my ass out. I was instructed to go down the block to my Grandmother's house, so that's exactly what I did.

A few days later, it was time to return to school. I went home and knocked on the door. My mom answered, but when I didn't say "Good morning," she slammed the door in my face. I knocked again and apologized. Only then did she allow me to enter. Inside, my clothes were laid out and my lunch was packed. She sent me on my way without as much as a single word.

I never played with fire again after that. That day taught me something I didn't even realize I was learning at the time: how to take responsibility for my mistakes and how to apologize even when the shame burns hotter than the flames. It's a childhood lesson that I've carried with me ever since.

Reader Reflection

Fire can destroy or reveal what's been hidden in the dark. Both happened in this chapter.

Before you turn the page, pause. Breathe. This is your space to sit with what still smolders inside you—the memories that seared your mind and heart, the lessons that left marks, and the light you found in the ashes.

What moments from your childhood still burn quietly inside you?

_____

_____

_____

_____

_____

_____

Who or what taught you to take responsibility before you were ready?

_____

_____

_____

_____

_____

_____

What lessons did you have to learn too early in life?

_____

_____

_____

_____

_____

_____

How do you carry your younger self's pain or shame today?

_____

_____

_____

_____

_____

_____

If you could speak to that younger version of yourself, what would you say?

Remember: Even in destruction, there's rebirth. You survived the flames—which means you were never meant to be consumed by them.

Chapter 4

Stormy Seasons & Side Streets

T he years between ten and twelve felt like a blur—confusion and chaos that moved like weather I couldn't predict. Every few steps felt like walking straight into another devastating storm. Many of those storms came at the hands of other people.

I remember lying in bed with a girl and her boy cousin who were both about the same age as me. It was some unspoken game we all seemed to know. I rolled between them—his hands, her hands— none of us understanding what we were doing, just that it felt grown and forbidden.

Looking back, I realize we were just kids acting out what had already been done to us. Maybe we'd all been touched improperly. Maybe we were trying to find language for our confusion. It came out as "play" because we didn't yet comprehend what sex was.

There was another girl in our building—five years older, bold, sure of herself. When our mothers hung out in the living room smoking and laughing, we had our own little "play dates" in her room. At first, it was just us playing with toys, watching tv, and eating snacks—kids stuff.

But she had this way of switching gears. like flipping a secret switch. One day, she told me straight up, "When I scream "apples" from the bathroom, come in and put your mouth on my breast." I remember standing there frozen, heart beating fast like a drum. But when the call came ,"Apples!", I went and did what I was told to do.

Crazy as it sounds, back then it all felt normal to me. It was like I was playing a role in a show that had been running long before I walked on stage. Case in point, I remember being left with a babysitter in my aunt's building. The lady and her brother were different—the kind of people that made your stomach turn. The odd pair made me sit on the brother's lap and kiss him on his nasty ass mouth. Same lap, same breath. It was like déjà vu—I couldn't escape. A sickening damn show on repeat, where the adults passed the *This is What We Do to Kids* script around.

Childhood innocence lost at the hands of predators. I also attribute it to my "run ins" with the cousins and the older girl. What happened between me and those kids wasn't necessarily a conscious choice. It was inherited confusion. 'Cause when pain doesn't get named, it turns into behavior. We were simply acting out the roles forced on us.

The preteen blur trickled over to middle school and high school. Days, weeks, months, and years just whirred by. Looking back, I think I was in autopilot mode, just trying to survive. Some of what transpired during that time is lost on me. But there are some memories that are etched in my head and heart forever.

Summer 1990 was the kind of hot that sticks to your skin. My little brother was born that June. My sister and I stayed at my

Grandmother's house while my mom was at the hospital giving birth. But after he arrived, we never went back home with my mother. It wasn't discussed, it just happened. One day became two. Two became months. And suddenly we lived there. Those years were hard. Imagine living so close to your mother but not being allowed to go back home with her. That ache never leaves. It just sits in your chest, heavy and still.

Time passed slowly. My mother visited about once a week, showing up like the wind—sometimes calm, sometimes wild. By then, I knew she was using drugs more often. Her light was dimmer and her smile wasn't as wide. But I still saw my mother behind the shell of who'd she become.

One Christmas, I had a little money in my pockets. I decided that I wanted to do something nice to make her smile. Even though my mother was still deep into her Jehovah's Witness ways, I bought her a gift—a makeup palette with about twenty-five shades. All bright, all loud—like her spirit used to be.

When I gave it to her, she lit up. She sat right in my Grandmother's living room and tried on every damn color. When she walked out she looked like *Whatever Happened to Baby* Jane—it was hilarious. Her face was a rainbow crime scene, but she wore it proudly. That was my mother—you had to love her exactly as she was.

The holidays came and went. Winter and Spring went by just as quickly. Next thing I knew, Summer was coming in fast and hot! Living with my Grandmother was an adjustment. Navigating kinship care took a toll on me. My behavior wasn't great and my attitude towards adults was disgusting. I'd curse my teachers out and get into fights with other students almost daily. Needless to say, my grades were terrible because I didn't care about learning at that point.

Real talk, I graduated by the skin of my teeth. It's a miracle that I graduated at all because during graduation rehearsal I refused to cooperate. I often failed to follow directions by doing the opposite of what was asked to me—thinking I was funny. In hindsight, I was also seeking attention. But at the end of the day, I goofed off one time too many and was kicked out of my sixth-grade graduation.

I felt like shit, especially because my friends and family made fun of me. I was the butt of their jokes and it didn't feel good. So, I made a promise to do better in middle school. I meant it too. I had something to prove—not only to my Grandmother or to the school, but to myself too. And for a while, I held up that promise.

Middle school started off well. I was excited for a fresh start. I was also happy that some of my friends from elementary school were there, so I felt safe. Straight out the gate, I was doing all of my classwork and homework. I was focused man!

That changed though when my Grandmother allowed me to get a pass to go out for lunch—that may have been the worst thing she could have done. I started making new friends and was slowly moving away from my familiar friends. I got semi-popular fast. Not on purpose, but because of my vibe—a little rough, funny, smart-mouthed, and quick with comebacks. I was the kind of person people either loved or hated—and I didn't care which.

The first few weeks of having a lunch pass, I'd go home, eat, and head back to school. That was my routine until one of my new friends invited me to her house. On the way there, we stopped at this weed spot on the hill near her building. She went inside and got weed from the old man. I knew what weed was but had never smoked it or wanted to for that matter. But since she was doing it, I decided to try it too. Soon, we were hanging out every day. Our routine was to stop at the weed spot before heading to her house to smoke, eat, and then go back to school. Needless to say, my weed habit was born.

Then, something strange happened. The girl disappeared and I never saw her again. I don't know what happened, but one day she was absent from school and never came back. That didn't stop me from following the routine though. Since the old man in the weed spot knew me, I figured I'd go in and try my luck. I was scared as hell, but I wanted to smoke and chill before going back to school. I mustered up the courage and went into the store. I wasn't expecting the conversation I had with the old dreadhead. He gave me the weed, but requested sex in return. I agreed to return after school to make due on my promise. But after smoking my weed and thinking hard about it, I knew I had to go home 'cause I wasn't trying to get a beating. In that moment, I decided I'd never go back to that store again.

Since my new friend wasn't around anymore, I began hanging out with another girl who would later become one of my kid's fathers' baby mother. She introduced me to cutting school, which was a whole different level from just cutting class. See, when you cut school, you can't go back in the building and you obviously can't go home. So, we had to stay outside all day until school was over. But this girl had a plan.

She introduced me to the weed spot on my block—we called it "Blue Door". You could only get weed from there if you knew how to knock on the door the correct way. She knew the knock, so we got our smokes without an issue. We were chilling in front of a store smoking when my Grandmother drove by in a cab. She screamed my name so loud, but the car never stopped. When I got home, I was in so much trouble. That was the last time I hung out with that girl.

Eventually, I connected with a girl who would become my best friend/sister. I'll never forget the day we met. I was in the staircase fighting my then boyfriend when God had her come through the exit. She immediately went into fight mode. We beat that boy's tail!!! We didn't see much of each other in the days after that. But it seemed like our friendship was built on fighting because the following week after the staircase incident, she was getting jumped by some girls and I jumped right in for her like she did for me. From that day on, we were together every day and had each other's back.

I managed to make it through the last year of middle school without much excitement—just the same ole cycle of cutting class, getting in trouble, and hanging with my friends. I even went to my senior prom. But of course, I had to have my last hoorah before my middle school exit.

We took a trip to an amusement park in Jersey for our senior trip. And me being me, far from just a regular kid had to go out with a bang—well, not intentionally. When it was time to head home, I insisted on one last ride, which ended up costing me and five of my friends our ride back. The bus left without us, so the police had to drive us to Port Authority. Broke and desperate, I tried calling home collect, but my Grandmother didn't accept the call. By some miracle, I found a quarter in a payphone and called her crying. I explained that they'd left us on purpose—unaware that the principal had already notified her of what exactly happened. Let's just say I walked straight into a well-deserved beating when I got home.

Nobody was happier than me when middle school was finally over. I made it to graduation which was a big deal because remember what happened in elementary school. Up next after middle school was high school. I chose one near Fordham Road in the Bronx. That neighborhood had its own heartbeat—fast, loud, and unpredictable. Just like me.

I was so happy when I found out that my best friend was attending the same school. It was like God threw us a bone. And when we locked eyes on campus, it was an instant: "back to business" energy.

We had it all mapped out. She'd catch the 41, I'd take the 15, and we'd meet at the 17 bus on Fordham Road and head to school. Other days, we'd just link on Fordham, grab a sandwich and disappear. We were never really in school—at least, not mentally.

Our first year was pure adventure. Cutting class. Ducking security. Fighting. Meeting boys. Switching blocks like we were on tour. We gave every corner a nickname. Our lives were a movie, and in our heads, we were the stars.

When we cut school, we went all over the place. One day, we ended up at a high school on Trinity Ave—and that's where I met my second-best friend. From that day on, the three of us became inseparable. Sisters—a bond that nobody could break.

The crazy part? We were complete opposites. I was the ghetto girl—sagging my pants, rocking a headscarf, and always ready for whatever. Lightskin was the pretty one with long hair, a nice, slim shape, and stood taller than me. And Brownskin had that smooth brown complexion, medium height, and was quiet but sneaky. She was the "church girl", but not really. Together though? We were the *IT* girls.

All the boys were drawn to us, and we were just young and dumb, following dudes around without a single thought about the risk. We could've been kidnapped, raped, or killed, but we didn't think about any of that because we were busy chasing vibes.

One time, we followed some older boys from Tremont to 183rd because they said there was a party poppin' off. No invites. No names. Just vibes. The "party" turned out to be a hot-ass living room with a broken fan and four dudes slouched on a couch passing around a blunt. We stayed five minutes, then dipped and laughed the whole way home.

Over time, we started hanging out around Webster Ave and 180th. The buildings in that neighborhood were built weird to me—some apartments had upstairs and downstairs and some were side-by-side with two front doors on each end. Either way, the guys we were messing with would let us come hang during school hours.

I remember one day clearly. The guys weren't letting us inside. I started crying and told them I had to pee, so they let us in—but said we couldn't go upstairs. As they walked us to the door, I jetted around one of the boys and shot straight upstairs. Two girls were laid up in the bed in the room. My friend and I beat them girls so badly. We dragged them out and threw all their shit into the hallway. But we kept their Walkmans.

There was no real reason for us fighting the girls, we just liked to fight back then. In hindsight, we should've whopped the boys' asses for being trifling. But those were the moments—the dumb, funny, and dangerous shit that made us feel alive.

As my first year of high school wound down and summer crept in, there were days we stayed in school just to chill. We spent hours in the Dean's office—it was right near the gym where the boys hung out and close to the bathrooms where we could sneak off to smoke cigarettes. My Grandmother received phone calls daily about me missing class or school altogether. Luck would have it on one particular day she didn't wait for the school to call her.

I guess her radar must've gone off, because I'd been absent more than I was present. By some twist of fate, I was actually in the Dean's office when the phone rang. I picked it up without thinking—just another dumb thing I'd do because it seemed fun and funny at the time.

"Hello?"

And then I heard my Grandmother's voice. And she caught my voice immediately—I don't know how, but she knew it was me. I slammed that phone down so fast out of shock and fear. How ironic was it that she called, and I picked up the phone? But hey, at least she couldn't say I wasn't in school.

Picking up that phone and hearing my Grandmother's voice on the other end wasn't what I expected, but it didn't scare me enough to stop me from cutting school. I just learned that I had to be more strategic about how I did it. I found a friend who absolutely loved school and told her to sign me in to homeroom and any classes that we had together so that it looked like I was in attendance. And just like that, the phone calls home stopped because according to attendance records, I was present at school.

Those were some wild days. Though challenging, I know now that my behavior was a reflection of the chaos of my life—sexual abuse, parental abandonment, drug use, peer pressure, poor decisions, etc. Life's storms led me to side streets filled with distractions, detours, and danger. By the grace of God, I survived it all.

Reader Reflection

The years that teach us the dangers of storms also teaches us how to survive them. This page is for the parts of you that navigated through stormy seasons, walked dark streets, and learned street codes—yet found your light in the midst of the chaos.

Write here—let it hold what you need to leave behind.

Where in your life have you ever felt like you were walking into one storm after another?

_____

_____

_____

_____

_____

_____

What "side streets" (Places, people, habits, or disguises.) did you take to feel safe, seen, or alive?

_____

_____

_____

_____

_____

_____

Who were your allies — the friends, the unexpected protectors, the people who showed up — and why did they matter?

_____

_____

_____

_____

_____

_____

Think about the line: *We gave every corner a nickname. Our lives were a movie, and in our heads, we were the stars.* What role did you play in your own story — rebel, protector, runaway, comedian, survivor?

_____

_____

_____

_____

_____

_____

What risky choices or escapes did you use to cope — and what did they cost you or teach you?

_____

_____

_____

_____

_____

If you could tell your adolescent self one steady truth before the next storm, what would it be?

_____

_____

_____

_____

_____

Remember: You learned to move through storms you weren't meant to navigate. That shows resilience—and it also deserves gentleness. Let this page be a witness to both.

Chapter 5

Unplugged

I wasn't a stranger to cutting school—in fact, I was a pro. I usually didn't think twice about it—I just did what I felt like doing regardless of the consequences. But there was that one time that I cut for a good reason.

It was the last few weeks of school. I was cutting one time for the road—but this time was different. Why? Because my mom asked, well told me to do it.

During one of our phone convos she told me the plan. I was expected to leave school at a certain time and meet her at a specific location. The fact that she had concocted a plan for me to play hooky with her was shocking because she didn't play about school. Ever. My punishment for anything I did wrong was reading the dictionary or the Encyclopedia front to back. She was serious about education in a way that felt unshakable.

By the time my mom devised our "hooky hangout", she had been working on getting clean and she was doing pretty well with her substance abuse treatment. She wanted to see me and spend time with me, which wasn't her usual thing. So, I was hype to leave school—no questions asked.

I remember walking out those school doors with my heart racing—half from excitement, half from curiosity. It wasn't like I was sneaking off to do something bad—I was going to see my mom. The streets felt different that day. The air was warmer and brighter, like it knew something important was about to happen.

When I met her, she smiled the way she used to when things were good—before the storms, the glassy eyes, and the yelling. She took me by the hand, and we started our little adventure. She showed me her drug program—a big, blue building in Harlem. People were hanging outside in clusters—some laughing, some lost in their own worlds. The air was thick with cigarette smoke and body odor.

She introduced me to a few people, but my attention was mainly focused on her. She had a glow on her face that day—not the same brightness from my early childhood, but enough to make me want to believe in her. After the introductions, she showed me her room. It was small, but it was hers. The bed was made, a chair sat by the window, and a little nightstand held her things. I tried to memorize everything—the way her clothes were folded, the faint smell of baby powder mixed with some chemical. If I never came back, at least I'd never forget my visit to her new home.

Afterwards, we went out to eat. I can't remember exactly what we had—maybe burgers or chicken—but I remember the feeling of sitting across from her and laughing. It felt good walking around Harlem too because it reminded me of the good ole days. Back when she'd send me on "missions," except this time we were doing it together.

When it was time for me to head home, she reached into her bag and handed me a wad of food stamps and told me to split it with my sister and brother. I nodded and tucked it away like a prized treasure. During her struggle, she made a way to provide for us, which meant a lot and was to be valued.

The summer rolled in and I was living. I had a bunch of boyfriends—nothing serious, just little flings that gave me a reason to go outside. Every time I ventured out, it was a movie. Music spilled out of windows. Kids played freeze tag on the corner. The sun turned sidewalks into hot plates you had to dance across.

When my cousin got her apartment in Castle Hill, I spent the rest of the summer there. Freedom. No cramped house. No constant rules. My cousin was cool—she had rules, but not the kind that made me feel trapped. We stayed up late watching TV, laughing, and eating whatever we wanted.

And then—the worst thing in the world happened.

One afternoon, the phone rang. My cousin answered. The look on her face told me before she even spoke that something was wrong. She said my mother was in the hospital. My stomach dropped. They told me she was fine and that I could see her the next day. The following day, my cousin took me to a hospital in Harlem. I remember walking through those sliding doors, the smell of antiseptic hitting me so hard it burned. The hallways were too white, too bright, and too cold.

And then I saw her.

My mother was lying in a hospital bed, hooked up to what seemed like a thousand machines—tubes everywhere. A breathing machine was doing the work her body couldn't. The beeping was steady, but it sounded like it was counting down to something.

My family was there—the ones close enough to come. And sitting across from me was him—the man my mother had introduced me to just weeks before. The one she'd been seeing romantically. I stared at him so hard, I swear I killed him a hundred times over and over in my head. Rage boiled inside me, but it was trapped under the blanket of shock.

The hospital said she'd had an aneurysm. They said it was triggered by a fight she'd had with him earlier that day—something about her head hitting the dresser in the room she lived in. While all the ways I could hurt him ran through my mind, the main thing I was thinking was: *Why is he here? Why is he sitting in this room with our family while she's lying there not breathing on her own?*

And then came the decision.

The doctors said there was no real chance she'd recover. The family talked about removing her from life support. I wanted to scream and throw myself in front of them to protest their decision. I was too young to understand the medical part, but I knew one thing—I wanted my mother alive. She was supposed to live forever. But sadly, she didn't.

On July 12, 1995, they unplugged her. And just like that, my mother—my best friend and my anchor—was gone.

I remember thinking my life was never going to have meaning again. Happiness wasn't meant for me anymore and I hated everybody. I especially hated everyone who chose to take her off that machine. My sister was too young to understand. My brother was too little to even remember her. And there I was, standing in the wreckage, trying to make sense of it all. That day, I made a promise to her in my heart—once I was old enough, I'd take my sister and brother and raise them myself. I didn't know how, but I knew I would.

Because of the trauma I experienced, my Grandmother and the foster care agency arranged for me to go to therapy. At first it was just counseling where you talk about your feelings. But when that didn't work, they put me into psychotherapy. Those rooms were cold in a different way than the ones at the hospital. I'd sit there with my arms crossed, trying to read the psychotherapist's face before saying anything. Some days I talked. Some days I didn't. Progress came in little drips, like a faucet you can't quite turn all the way on.

To this day, losing my mother impacts me. I think about all the things we didn't get a chance to do together. And how she never got the chance to meet her grandchildren. The memories and the what ifs left a gaping hole in my heart that can never be plugged.

Reader Reflection

Some endings don't come with warning signs—just silence, a flicker, and then the sound of everything you love being unplugged. This page is for the pieces of you that learned what loss really feels like, for the child who had to grow up overnight, and for the adult still learning how to breathe again after the storm.

When was the first time you truly understood loss?

_____

_____

_____

_____

_____

What did "goodbye" look or feel like for you?

_____

_____

_____

_____

_____

_____

Think about the line: *On July 12, 1995, they unplugged her.* What moment in your life felt like everything changed in a single breath?

_____

_____

_____

_____

_____

_____

How did grief manifest itself (silence, anger, strength, etc.)?

_____

_____

_____

_____

_____

_____

If you could sit with the person you lost—what would you want them to know and why?

_____

_____

_____

_____

_____

_____

Remember: Love doesn't die when someone you love takes their last breath—it just finds new ways to live inside you.

Chapter 6

Searching for Love

After my mother's passing, I was heartless and careless. The last two months of summer consisted of me meeting boys—that was my way of coping. It was a distraction—and in some ways, being with boys made me feel whole and complete. Despite losing my mom, I had a pretty decent summer. But I was ready to get back into my books.

I could barely sleep the night before the first day of school—I was too excited. To set the vibe, I popped my favorite tape in the cassette player—Biggie's *Ready to Die* was my "get-up-and-go" album. After finding my favorite song, I showered, dressed, and tied a scarf on my head because I never did my hair. When I looked in the mirror to check my outfit, something didn't look right.

"Your body's filling out, girl," I thought to myself. I had on my cute, tight red Levi's, a snug black shirt, and my 54-11s—black with a red bandana. "Nah, that hair gotta be done. The boys are checking for

45

you more now. Get your hair right!" So, I brushed my hair into a feathered ponytail and went on my way.

The second year of high school was gonna be a breeze. My boyfriend was a block boy. He had a little money and he kissed good. I had money for my hair and my snacks. What more could a girl ask for?

I headed to the 17 bus which took me straight to my school. My best friend was late as usual, so we agreed to meet in the lunchroom. Walking into school, I passed the security booth feeling a little nervous. Summer had introduced me to gang life. I was never in a gang, but I had learned how to spit a razor blade like a pro. Keeping a blade in your mouth was the easiest way to have a weapon without getting caught. I thought the security guards would stop me, but nope, I was in.

Straight to the lunchroom I went, waiting on my bestie. I grabbed breakfast, 'cause those English muffins and chocolate milk were everything. I found a table near the front, even though all the cool kids sat in the back. Feet kicked up on a chair, stuffing my face, when in walked the coolest security guard in the school. She walked over, pushed my feet off the chair, and said, "Loosen the button on those pants—you're suffocating that baby!"

"What are you talking about?" I said.

A smirk crept across her face.

"You know what I'm talking about."

"I'm NOT pregnant!" I snapped.

Let's be clear—I was not a virgin. I even had a sex calendar that me and my bestie made so that I could keep track of who I gave it to. But that got old quick, so I decided to stop checking for all the hustlers on the block. I cut my rotation down to Drugga—we started sleeping together before my fifteenth birthday. In my mind, we were in a relationship, even though we were never together in public.

Drugga and I never used protection. So, later that day, I spoke with my therapist about the conversation I'd had with the security guard. She asked if I wanted to take a pregnancy test and I said yes. Sure enough, it came back positive.

I was so confused when I left her office. I went straight to see Drugga and told him I was pregnant—at the top of that the same roof where I think the baby was conceived. "Who's the father?" he asked. His reaction didn't surprise me because he knew I was sleeping with a couple of other people. The disappointment of being pregnant and getting that reaction came with an even bigger blow (literally) when I got home. My Grandmother had already been informed about my pregnancy. I was met with a slap across the face.

I couldn't believe my Grandmother hit me—but what hurt worse was that my therapist betrayed me by calling her. Even at that age, I knew that she wasn't supposed to disclose what we talked about during our sessions. She'd told me and my Grandmother that during the consultation. Obviously, her word didn't mean anything, so that was my last therapy session.

The weeks ahead were stressful. There was no discussion about how we should handle my pregnancy. My Grandmother simply made an appointment for me to get an abortion. My cousin took me to the clinic, but when the doctors described the procedure, I started crying and saying, "I don't want to do it."

My cousin took me home, but my Grandmother insisted that I go through with it. So, my aunt took me back to the clinic. But, by then, I was five months pregnant and the doctor refused to perform the procedure. I had so many mixed emotions. I'd lie on my stomach to try and cause a miscarriage, but that didn't work. Two minutes later, I'd change my mind and want to keep my baby.

My family was so upset about my pregnancy. To the point that they never spoke about it or even asked how I was feeling. Christmas was right around the corner and my stomach was huge. The baby moved a lot, which was a new feeling. One day, I made a store run for my Grandmother, but I made a detour to see if I could spot Drugga. I wasn't prepared for what I saw when I turned the corner of my aunt's building. He was with a girl whose stomach was just as big as mine!

I wanted to stop and confront him, but I kept it moving. My thoughts raced: *She's pregnant? Who is she? Why didn't he speak? Why didn't I speak?* It didn't even matter—my soul told me to just leave it alone.

I attended my doctor visits alone—a reminder that my alleged baby father and I weren't in a relationship. All I could think was that this man really had a girlfriend—and she was pregnant too. As my February due date approached, I didn't know what to expect. I practiced breathing and pushing, but I was scared. Would I die? Could I do this? Was I strong enough?

The day after Valentine's Day, I went into labor. My aunt helped deliver my first child—KJ—in the ambulance in front of our building. He was 7 pounds, 12 ounces, with a cone-shaped head and the loudest cry I'd ever heard. On February 15, 1996, I became a mother for the first time. Even though my aunt hadn't been happy about the pregnancy, she helped me deliver and name him.

Everyone wanted to meet my little bundle of joy. But the only person I could think about was his father. A month after his birth, I saw Drugga in my aunt's building. When the elevator doors opened, he peeked into the stroller—but said nothing. The awkward, silent ride felt like forever. When I got off, I cried in the hallway before heading home.

Drugga never made any effort to see my child. I guess he thought I was content being a single mom. Thankfully, I loved my baby enough for the both of us. The next few months were easier. Summer was approaching and I was back outside, moving like I'd never left. Men wanted me even more now that I was pushing a stroller. Crazy enough, I was back to sleeping with Drugga.

Aside from messing around with him, I was caught up with old flings and a few new ones—I was happy. Then, I got the biggest surprise of my life—I was pregnant again. This time, I wasn't sure who the father was. From my calculations, the only possible option was Drugga. Again.

Having another baby by him when he wasn't taking care of the first one was crazy. But I went through the pregnancy alone—again. I didn't expect anything from him; I already knew he wasn't going to step up. My days and nights blended together while I tried to care for a young baby, prepare for a new one, and stay sane all at the same time.

Before I knew it, it was my son's first birthday. To celebrate, I threw him a party at my Grandmother's house. I was walking around hosting when out of nowhere, I felt a sharp pain in my stomach. I tried to ignore it and continued hosting. But my Grandmother's best friend noticed that I was having trouble walking and screamed through the house that I was in labor. Labor or not, I was determined not to leave my son's party before the birthday song. As soon as we sang "Happy Birthday," I called the ambulance and grabbed a slice of cake for the ride.

My aunt accompanied me again, and just like before, things escalated fast. The hospital sent me home, but within an hour, I was in full-blown labor. My son Trey was born on February 16, 1997—on my aunt's couch, with the umbilical cord wrapped around his neck. Maybe that's why he's such a couch potato now, lol. It's only by the grace of God that both of my kids were born outside of a hospital and each of us survived.

After two babies by the same man who didn't pay us any mind, you'd think I would've learned my lesson. But I didn't. All I knew was how to use men and the system. I felt that controlling men through sex was how I took back my power from those who'd once abused me. But eventually, I realized I wasn't going to find love or redemption with my vagina. I needed to learn how to love myself—and I did...until I didn't again.

Reader Reflection

Love can be both the wound and the medicine. Sometimes we go searching for it in every place it once hurt us, trying to rewrite the story—to prove we were always worth staying for.

This page is your pause—your mirror—to look at what love has meant to you, how it's shaped you, saved you, and sometimes broken you.

When did you first confuse attention with love?

_____

_____

_____

_____

_____

What did love look like for you when you didn't yet love yourself?

_____

_____

_____

_____

_____

_____

Think about the line: *I came to a realization that I wasn't going to find love or redemption with my vagina.* Where have you searched for love in places that only gave you pain?

_____

_____

_____

_____

_____

_____

Who or what taught you the difference between being wanted and being valued?

_____

_____

_____

_____

_____

_____

How do you practice loving yourself now—differently, or more gently—than before?

_____

_____

_____

_____

_____

_____

If your younger self could see you now, what do you think she'd say?

_____

_____

_____

_____

_____

_____

_____

_____

_____

_____

_____

_____

_____

Remember: You deserve the kind of love you give to others.

Chapter 7

Roses, Lies, and Sidewalks

I was still living at my Grandmother's house with my two children—it was getting more crowded by the day though. It became hard for me to sleep in the bed with both of them, so I decided to get on public assistance using my aunt's address out in Staten Island. It was easier that way because someone in my Grandmother's house was already receiving benefits, so I couldn't use that address without messing things up. The plan was to go into the shelter, but honestly, I was nervous. Instead, I stayed at my Grandmother's house and collected my money from the system.

I used all of my food stamps to buy groceries to help out—adding to whatever my Grandmother already brought in. I bought my own toiletries and whatever else my kids needed. I never wanted to ask anyone for anything. It was important for me to be as independent as possible and not be a burden to my family.

I only went to Staten Island when I had appointments or when the social workers came for home visits to make sure I was living there. For whatever reason, I ended up sleeping with Drugga again. I remember him coming all the way out to Staten Island to see me. My family had gone to some sort of celebration so I was home with my kids. It was late when he showed up, so the kids were asleep on the couch. Of course he didn't acknowledge them, although every time I gave myself to him I secretly wished that he would be a father to our children.

My aunt lived in a small studio apartment on Clove Road, tucked inside of a little building. Me and Drugga had a quick sex session on her bed—I know, the nerve. I swear it couldn't have been five minutes later when my three aunts walked through the door. He wasn't even dressed and I had to think fast. I told him to jump into the bathtub.

As soon as my aunt—the one who lived there—walked in, she went straight to the bathroom. I was shook! I stood there in the doorway talking to her the whole time trying to figure out how to get this man out without anybody noticing so that I wouldn't get in trouble. I ran through every possible plan in my head where he could exit the bathroom and make a beeline out the front door (which was just across the hall—thank God) without being seen.

As soon as she finished using the bathroom, I followed her into the kitchen. That's when I saw the pamper I had thrown in the trash earlier—and boom—that was the plan! I grabbed the pamper and acted like I was just taking out the garbage. While she and my other aunts were distracted in the kitchen, we moved quick as hell. Somehow, we pulled it off and didn't get caught.

That went on all throughout the summer. We'd meet up whereever—stairwells, parks, random corners—do our business, then go our separate ways like nothing ever happened. No feelings.

No expectations—other than me secretly wishing he'd step up as a dad. But as they say, "You can't make a man want to be a dad."

Spring of 1998, I'm walking down the block on Park Ave and 170th Street with one child in the stroller and the other one sitting on the hood of it. No destination—just walking aimlessly, taking in the sights and sounds. Another regular day of getting my kids dressed and walking around the neighborhood until my feet were tired.

I was a week post-op from having my very first abortion and was just thinking about life and how I ended up in that predicament. I wasn't even sure who the father was, but I knew I wasn't having another baby, especially without knowing who the daddy was.

Walking down the street minding my business, when a little two-door silver car filled with a bunch of men passes me, then stops short. The car backs up. I instantly think I'm about to get shot or have to fight—because I'm from the hood, and if a car does that, that's usually how it ends.

But nah. A big Black man jumps out of the driver's seat.

"Yo, Ma!" he called.

I'm like, "What?" with all kinds of don't-fuck-with-me attitude.

He says, "Yo, why you so hostile?"

I replied, "Why you jumping out on me like that?"

With a rose in his hand, he says, "I just wanted to give you a flower because it's Mother's Day." As flattered as I was, I didn't even realize it was Mother's Day. I had never had the pleasure of celebrating it, even though I was a mother of two. I took his flower and said, "Thanks," then proceeded to walk off.

He shouted, "Yo, where you going? Can I get your number?"

Now, for several reasons, I didn't like talking to men in cars. But he was charming—about six feet tall, roughly 250 pounds, and had a nice, crooked smile. It even looked like he talked with his tongue a little—one of those weird things I liked in men. So I gave him my number. With attitude, I also took his. The only problem was I didn't have a phone—I had given him the number to my Grandmother's house phone. So, I wouldn't know if he called unless I was home.

After running the streets all day with my two little boys, I finally made my way home. I was living with my Grandmother, my aunt and her two children, my other cousin, my sister, and my brother in a three-bedroom apartment in the projects on Washington Ave. Talk about a full house!

When I got in, I was greeted with, "A guy named Tee called for you." I was hyped he called, but didn't want to show it. I checked the caller ID, got his number, and called him back. The first thing he said was, "What are you doing tonight?"

"I just got home," I said.

He asked, "You wanna go out?"

As much as I wanted to, I had no one to watch my children. He said, "I'll pay someone if you can get them to babysit." So, I asked my aunt, even though we never really liked each other. She was—and still is—about her money, so she agreed.

When Tee came to the house later that night, he asked to speak to my aunt in order to pay her. She came to the door, told him the price, and he paid her on the spot. One thing you will learn about me—I like a man with a few dollars—so I knew he was gonna be around for a while.

Our date was cute. Movie, dinner, and a trip to the hotel. I had never been to a hotel, so I was feeling like a queen. The place was right off the Hutchinson Parkway in the Bronx. It had mirrors on the ceiling and a nice jacuzzi (which we actually used). Sitting between his legs in the hot tub, talking and laughing, I felt like I was in a music video.

When we got out, the worst thing happened though. My ponytail got caught on his chain. I walked out that hottub baldheaded, with my fake hair dangling from his chain. I was embarrassed, but he didn't care. We got to business and I left that place happy.

On the ride home, slow jams played. Guilt started to creep in about leaving my boys for so long. In front of my building, he kissed me good night and handed me some money. I didn't look at it or count it, but I knew from experience—this man did this a lot. After any "session" with a man that had no real interest in you came funds. I thought, *He probably has a thousand girls because he knows exactly what to do. This ain't gonna work... but I'm gonna take this little bit of money and go on my way.*

Over the next few months, Tee and I met up twice a week. It started to feel like we were in a relationship. It was never discussed, but the consistency made me think so. Then boom—one day I called his house and a girl answered. I had met all his friends, male and female, so I knew she wasn't just a friend. She sounded like she had just woken up. I asked to speak to him, and she said he wasn't home. With a bit of anger in my heart, I hung up.

Then I called back and asked who she was. She told me she was his girlfriend. My heart dropped. Tears fell without warning. I hung up again. This time, she called me back asking who I was. I said, "I'm his girlfriend." Silence—the kind that feels like forever.

We finally broke the silence and agreed that I'd meet her at his house. I told my family that I was taking one of my son's toys back to Toys "R" Us because it was broken. I didn't take the boys though, in the event that this girl wanted to fight. But I took my little brother with me to make it look like I was really just going to the store and coming right back. He was old enough to know how to stay out of the way if anything happened. Even though I knew this girl didn't care about this man cheating, I wanted to fight. And I wanted to fight both of them.

When I got there, she was nice. She let me in, wearing his shirt as pajamas. I wanted to take her head off, but I stayed cool. We talked. She knew exactly what he was doing—she had been through this with him before.

She even tried to prove to me how much of a cheater this man was by showing me the sex tapes that he made in that same apartment with other women. The more I watched, the angrier I got. We were about twenty minutes into the second tape when she called him to see how close he was. When he confirmed that he was parking his car, my brother and I hid in his bathroom—in the shower—because it was a studio apartment.

When he came in, she started asking about me. He denied everything—until I came out of the shower. It was a shit show! When I suddenly emerged, he looked shocked and started saying he had broken up with me and that I was stalking him. I was so heartbroken I didn't even care to fight. I just wanted to go home and cry. That walk back home from 135th and 5th Ave to 170th and Washington Ave felt like a lifetime. I couldn't cry in front of my brother, so my head and my heart just pounded the whole way home.

As much as I wanted that to be the end, he sucked me back in with apologies and lies. And even though I knew they were lies, I didn't care. Besides, I had met another guy. Same way too—I was walking up 170th, making my way to Jerome Ave for no reason—just needed to walk. He stopped me. Not my usual type. I liked a big, husky man. This guy was slim, dark-skinned, tall—well, taller than me. But he was cute, so I stopped.

I gave him my Grandmother's house number, he gave me his beeper number, and we went our separate ways. Like every other guy, he called that same day and asked me to come outside to chill.

I took my boys with me and we hung on the stoop almost all night. I watched him sell drugs like it was nothing. He fed me and the kids, then sent us home in a cab.

No sex or money transaction. In my mind, I thought, *this is strange— he must be gay or something.* It didn't take long for him to prove me wrong. We started sleeping together which made me happy because I knew Tee was still engaging other women, so it was my turn to have fun. This "relationship" started out just like any other— with consistency—and my dumb ass, always in my head and heart, thinking I was in a relationship. But this time was a little different because I had two men—and I was happy and content.

Reader Reflection

Sometimes "love" shows up in the form of a lie, holding a rose. It smells sweet, looks soft, but the thorns always remind you what it costs to pick it up.

This chapter was full of motion—walking, chasing, returning, pretending—but underneath it all was a heart still learning what it meant to be wanted versus being chosen.

This page is your space to slow down and face the truth beneath the noise.

When have you mistaken someone's attention for love?

_____

_____

_____

_____

_____

What red flags did you ignore because you wanted to believe in the fantasy?

_____

_____

_____

_____

_____

Think about the line: *As much as I wanted that to be the end, he sucked me back in with apologies and lies.* What's something you've had to walk away from more than once before you walked for good?

_____

_____

_____

_____

_____

Who or what have you given chance after chance to—even when you knew better?

_____

_____

_____

_____

_____

How do you know now when something real is standing in front of you?

_____

_____

_____

_____

_____

If you could go back and whisper one truth to your younger self, what would it be?

_____

_____

_____

_____

_____

Remember: You were always enough, even when others didn't realize it. Love begins with self-love—let it bloom wildly.

Chapter 8

Concrete Battles

S ummer was good—I juggled two men and enjoyed hanging out with my friends. I was carefree, unbothered, and both "relationships" were going well. 'Cause I could care less what either of those men were doing because I was getting what I needed from both of them.

Tee would come and pick me up when I needed to get away from my crowded house and needed some time away from my children. Slim was within walking distance for the days I didn't want to be with Tee or when I just wanted to be on the block chilling with him. I wasn't even sure where Slim lived, but we would frequent his sister's house just to hang out, or end up in hotel rooms or at his aunt's house in Harlem, where he had a room for us to do our business. And of course, both men made sure I never went home empty-handed or hungry. Being with Slim was a plus because he'd give me money just for me, and money to spend on my kids.

65

As Fall approached, staying at my Grandmother's house with my children and all my relatives was becoming stressful. When I told Slim what was going on, he offered me a place to stay. But, of course, it came with a lot of shit—that never fails with me and men, lol. It was his girlfriend's house, so in order for me and my kids to stay there, I had to be his "cousin."

As much as that hurt, I didn't want to go back home to my Grandmother, so I went along with it. When we got to the house, I noticed she was a slightly older woman—had to be in her mid-forties. She opened the door and welcomed me and my kids in. Then, she introduced me to her children, who were a little older than mine. Thankfully, they weren't Slim's kids. She told me I could sleep in the living room, so my children and I slept on the couch while he went into the bedroom with her. I'm sure they had sex with me in the other room. I cried all night.

The next morning, she went to work and took her kids to school. Slim was still sleeping. My kids and Slim's son were asleep as well. But as soon as Slim knew she was far enough away, he came to the living room to get me. We went back to that lady's room and had sex on her bed. To make matters worse, my menstrual came down in the middle of it. So not only did I violate this woman's trust—I violated her bed. I felt bad and guilty... but not enough to leave him alone.

I told Slim I never wanted to do that again, then went back home to my Grandmother's house. After that, I just rotated between Slim and Tee. This went on all winter. I would go to Slim's aunt's house in Harlem where he had a small room. When he'd leave, I'd put my children in the bed with me. I appreciated that he understood that we were a package deal.

The winter seemed short and fast. Before long, spring turned into summer. Slim and I were meeting up more frequently. It was mostly for the vibes because I loved going to Harlem. Even though his aunt's house was crowded, it was different.

I wasn't new to the drug game, but it was in his aunt's house that he actually showed me how to make crack, break it down, and bag it up. Him showing me that made me feel special—until his other baby mother wanted her time. I knew about her, but the way we were spending time together, I honestly thought he was done with her. The truth was, he was sleeping with both of us. I didn't care much because I was sleeping with him and someone else, so my feelings weren't hurt.

I was mad though that I had to leave the house. He sent me home on the train, and that's when I knew we were done. He could've put me in a cab—but instead he sent me on the train with my two children. That was a no-no. And yes, I felt entitled to a cab ride. Because he tried to play me out, I left him alone for a while and was just dealing with Tee.

And just as sure as my name is Sequoia, I was anticipating another great birthday—but it came with a baby bump yet again. My pregnancy went by fast—Tee was there for the whole thing. I ran into Slim once during my pregnancy near his sister's house. He was coming out of the bakery with a short Hispanic girl. When he saw me and my belly, he rubbed my stomach with excitement like he knew this was his child—and I went right along with it.

On February 5, 1999, I gave birth to my third son. When Tee came to visit me at the hospital, he made it clear that he wanted a blood test—and he had good reason. I didn't think he knew about Slim, but I'm sure he wasn't anybody's fool. Despite not knowing who the father was, I gave my son Tee's last name even though he never signed the birth certificate. I don't know what I was thinking.

At the ripe age of nineteen, I had three sons. Life wasn't no walk in the park. Some days felt like I was dragging myself along concrete, barefoot. One of the hardest things I ever had to deal with was not knowing who the father of my child was. That's a different kind of pain—a different kind of shame. I got so tired of comparing face cards—squinting at my baby's nose or ears to see if they matched somebody's family.

It wasn't even about lying—it was about surviving. I leaned more toward the one with the job because I wanted my son to be taken care of. I had already tasted what it felt like to be ignored—to watch Drugga walk past the children we made together and not even glance in their direction. That type of rejection stays with you. And Tee was sending me money orders every week and stopping by to see my son when he could—or when he wanted to. Slim, on the other hand, was nowhere in the picture.

As "luck" would have it, I'd spend the next few years running in and out of the shelter system. I was everywhere: the Bronx, Brooklyn, Queens, Manhattan, even Staten Island. Life was chaotic. Bags always packed. Hope always low.

Eventually, I got lucky. I was finally deemed eligible for a Tier 2 placement—one step closer to getting my own apartment. They placed me in the Bronx, over on 181st and Crotona Park South. It was close to my old block. Close to my old high school. A familiar kind of chaos.

I stayed in the shelter for a couple of months. Things were going well. The shelter had a daycare in the basement and classes we could take to get a certification. At the time, I thought I wanted to be an interior designer, but that quickly went out the window. So I enrolled in a GED program near the Lambert Houses. I tried to stay focused, but I ended up hanging out with some of the people in my class—some of them were from the block. That's where I met most of the boys. They were from a building we called the 800.

Being in school and having a taste of what it would be like to have my own place had me feeling like a real grown-up mother and it felt amazing. I cooked meals for my kids every night—Sunday dinner was my favorite: fried chicken, rice, collard greens, candied yams, and cornbread. We'd sit at the table and eat dinner as a family—I was so proud. My efforts didn't go unnoticed either. The people at the shelter conducted room checks and because my room was always spotless, I'd get certificates for having the cleanest room in the building. I'd be in that room on my knees scrubbing the floors, so I was happy that my labor wasn't in vain. More importantly, I was happy that I was creating a good home environment for my children.

While in the shelter system, I met a girl who also had three kids. We clicked immediately. Ironically, she lived on the other side of the street from Tee. One day, while I was visiting her, I met Courtland— he seemed like the big man on the block. He and I instantly hit it off—I'd visit him and he'd come see me in the shelter.

Tee and I were having our normal issues and he had a girlfriend. I could care less because I was doing my thing too. I'd met plenty of men while still dealing with Tee—one being the Courtland Ave dude. He was taller than me, maybe 200-250 pounds, really dark-skinned, dressed nice, and always smelled amazing. He reminded me of Biggie Smalls. I had also met an older man while walking to my aunt's house one day. He was driving a limo—tall, slim, brown-skinned, and really funny. So yeah, I was preoccupied. I didn't care about Tee or Slim for that matter.

Courtland and I were in a real relationship. He made it clear I was his girl. When I came to that block, everyone knew—and that was the validation I was looking for.

Even though I didn't need anyone else, the old man had a purpose. He had his own apartment—which was always clean—and I was welcome anytime. He gave me my first driving lessons with no license and even let me drive his Chevy Impala. That car was fast as hell, but he let me drive it like it was mine.

Too bad I couldn't drive it fast as hell from the storm that was brewing. Time was moving fast, but life was good. My third son was now eight months old and my children were well cared for. Things were going great until tragedy hit me like a Mack truck.

I knew my Grandmother had cancer. I had even escorted her to some of her appointments while I was pregnant with my third child. But I was never prepared to hear that she had passed away. I remember getting the call from my aunt—there was silence at first, then all I could hear were cries and sniffling. "She's gone. Mommy passed away," my aunt repeated a couple of times before the scream came out of my mouth. My life shifted again. I lost yet another piece of me.

The funeral was arranged and we laid my Grandmother to rest on November 3, 1999. I swear, at her burial I could hear her screaming, *Don't put me in here.* Maybe that was just my mind wishing she hadn't left me.

I was really sad for a long time. I wasn't in a good space and didn't want to be bothered much. But I kept in contact with Tee's mom— we talked regularly. One day, while cleaning, I was on the phone with her. Now that I think about it, I feel like she set me up. She asked me to come over with the baby—her alleged grandchild—and my other boys so we could cook dinner and enjoy it together. Knowing that her son and I weren't on the best terms and that we were in the middle of a paternity test, I went anyway.

When I got there, I started cleaning the chicken I was preparing to fry. Tee's family—his mother, niece, and sister—were playing with my kids and their "new addition" to the family. Then, Tee showed up at the door. I heard his mom tell him that I was there. I figured he might drop by. The issue was that he wasn't alone—he showed up with his new girlfriend.

We started arguing. He told me to get out of his mother's house and began pulling on me and my children. Everyone was frantic and screaming. Things were happening fast and tensions were heightened all because he was mad that I was visiting his mother. I also think he was showing out for his girlfriend, but that's another story.

Now, mind you, this man had just come out of the hospital after being stabbed up by some men over another female. Yet, he was in my face acting aggressively and trying to intimidate me. I was in the middle of cleaning the chicken, so I still had the knife in my hand. All I remember was him handing my son to his girlfriend and blocking me from getting to my baby while chaos broke out. His mother, nieces, and my other children were all screaming and pulling on both of us. I was just trying to fight my way through him to get to my baby. When I felt like I had no more strength left and realized I was hurting my child, I let go—and the next sixty seconds went black.

I remember calling my aunt and cousin to come help me. Before I knew it, there were police everywhere. When they asked if I stabbed him in front of my kids, I said, "Yes, look how big this man is—I was defending myself."

The next words pierced my soul: *"Put your hands behind your back, please. You have the right to remain silent..."* I had never been arrested before. I screamed, "For what?!" My sons were pulling on the cops, yelling for them to let me go. But their pleas fell on deaf ears as I was handcuffed and led away.

I thought it would just get swept under the rug. Nope. It turned into three years of straight fuckery. While I was sitting in a jail cell, my children were being put into the foster-care system without my knowledge.

Now, let me rewind to about a month before that incident to provide you with a bit more context. One day, I was taking care of my household chores, cleaning and doing laundry. On the way home from the laundromat with my three children—one in the stroller, one walking, and one sitting on top of the stroller—the unimaginable happened. I put the laundry supplies on top of the stroller. Unbeknownst to me, bleach was leaking down on my youngest child. I heard him crying but wasn't sure why. When I realized, I stopped immediately, rearranged everything, and kept going home. Once I got home, I immediately gave him a bath and made sure he was good. He didn't have any marks or anything that made me think I needed to take him to the doctor, even though that's exactly what I should have done.

Fast forward back to the arrest—it came with them saying I burned my son and that the kids were in danger, so they needed to be removed from my care. Now I was in court for an assault charge along with neglect—not even child abuse, just neglect. Fuck my life!

Reader Reflection

Some lessons don't come from classrooms or quiet moments—they come from the concrete.

From the weight of what you've carried, the love that cut too deep, and the choices that left bruises on your soul.

This chapter was survival in motion—raw, unfiltered, and full of truth. You learned that even when the world labels you a fighter, you were just trying to protect what little peace you had left.

What does survival look like for you today—not the fighting kind, but the peaceful kind?

_____

_____

_____

_____

_____

_____

Think about the line: *At the ripe age of nineteen, I had three sons. Life wasn't no walk in the park. Some days felt like I was dragging myself along concrete barefoot.* What moments in your life made you feel like that—tired, scraped, but still moving?

_____

_____

_____

_____

_____

_____

When did survival start feeling like a prison instead of protection?

_____

_____

_____

_____

_____

_____

You've carried guilt and blame that weren't all yours. What part of that story are you ready to forgive yourself for?

_____

_____

_____

_____

_____

_____

Who or what helped you get back up after you thought life had written you off?

_____

_____

_____

_____

_____

_____

If you could tell your nineteen-year-old self one thing she could hold onto through it all, what would it be?

_____

_____

_____

_____

_____

Remember: You're not defined by your concrete battles— you're defined by the way you learned to grow through the cracks.

Chapter 9

Stripped Bare

T hey said I burned him—that was the charge. But that was far from the truth—I didn't burn my son. To this day, I swear that I don't have any idea how he got that mark on his back. The only explanation I could think of was the bleach. But even that didn't make sense because the bleach had been dripping toward his face. Maybe somehow it ran down his back while it was on top of the stroller. Not only was it a mystery to me, I couldn't understand how or where the charge came from. 'Cause when I dropped the kids off at daycare, nobody—no counselor, no childcare worker, not one single person—ever said anything to me about my children's welfare. Yet those were my charges—child endangerment.

Sitting in that cell at central booking had me so stressed. There were like a thousand prostitutes in there—recruiting other women to work for their pimps. Of course, there were arguments galore. And fights broke out every time you turned around. It was pure chaos!

In the middle of all that foolishness, I caught my period. I had never been to jail before, so I didn't know what to expect. I called for the Correction Officer and asked for a pad. This bitch laughed in my face and said, "Do you know where you are? We don't give pads in here." Right then, I knew I couldn't stay in that place. What kind of world doesn't give a bleeding woman a pad? The fuck!

One prostitute—probably thinking if she helped me I'd let her recruit me—showed me how to create a makeshift pad from tissue. I was embarrassed and annoyed at the same time. I wrapped half the damn roll of tissue around my hand until it was thick enough, then stretched it out for length. It was a whole damn project. Out in the world, we don't think twice about these little things. But in there, shit gets real.

When I went to court the next day, the judge was going to set bail. But Tee's family was there advocating for me not to go to jail, so I was released. I still had to go to court for both the assault and the child neglect charge.

After my first few court dates, the case with my children was founded—meaning they had reason to believe that I burned my child—so my two oldest were placed in kinship care with my aunt. My youngest son was still with the dumb-ass who got me locked up. I had to call his phone, praying he'd accept the call so I could check on my child. I hated having to deal with him! And when he did answer, his girlfriend was always in the background—taking care of my son, being malicious, making sure I heard her voice. I cried after every call.

We finally got a date for the blood test. When it came back showing that my son wasn't his, I was relieved. Excited, even. That meant no more torture and no more phone calls where he held that power over me. Just like that, my chapter with him was done! Now, all of my children were back under one roof, living with my aunt who was their foster parent.

The staff at the family shelter had so much faith that I'd get my kids back. They even kept me on the resident list although I technically wasn't a family unit anymore. The women I bonded with there— women who admired my parenting, who trusted me with their kids—wrote letters to the judge on my behalf. They were supportive in a way that I didn't even expect.

During that time, I leaned on the men around me more than I should have. Courtlandt was the one who really showed up. He was there for everything and I was grateful. But not having my kids every day gave me a twisted sense of freedom. And when that freedom hit, I lost my mind. I was outside running the streets with no care in the world.

The old man seemed to back off. I saw him when I needed a place to sleep, but that was about it. I didn't care though because I was entertaining other men. One day, I was hanging out in front of the 800 with the people I'd gone through the GED program with. That's where I met someone who stood out—funny, independent, and carried himself differently. JJ was a tall, slim, dark-skin man with a witty personality. He was a nice man overall. He'd come see me at the shelter because he hustled right across the street. And he made sure to bring me food every night before he went home. Sometimes I'd get overnight passes just to spend the night at his house.

Even though I may have seemed happy to others, dealing with all these men was taking a toll on me. I was becoming drained— emotionally and physically. Not to mention I had started sleeping with Drugga again. He would also come to the shelter to see me. I know the security guards at that shelter were thinking all types of things about me—shit, I even tried to get one of the guards to come to my room to sleep with him, but he had morals and shut me down.

All of the "fun" I was having with these men caught up to me. I ended up getting pregnant again and absolutely had no clue who the father was. So, I did what I knew was best for me. I had my second abortion. I needed to do something different because this wasn't how I wanted to live my life.

One thing life is gonna do is life. I'd been through enough storms (sexual abuse, loss & grief, toxic relationships, etc.) to know that truth first hand. After a year of the caseworkers fighting and advocating to hold my spot in the family shelter, I was forced to leave. They put me out with no resources or any guidance. And even with all the men I was sleeping with and interacting with, no one could—or would—offer me a place to stay. At that point, I had no one. My family wasn't really there either. It was just me, Sequoia, out in the world fighting blindfolded. No direction. No guidance. Nothing.

The heartache of foster agency visits broke me. I hated it with a passion. I hated seeing my kids for just an hour with strangers hovering around. I hated that when I left they cried. After our visits, I'd wander the streets crying. I felt like I had failed everything and everyone. And no matter how many men I had around me, none of them could ever fill the void of not having my children.

After a year of being homeless (couchsurfing), I finally swallowed my pride and called my aunt. She was the only person I knew who didn't care what your situation was because she'd open her door regardless. She didn't want money or anything in return. All she asked was that you keep her house clean and keep whatever space she gave you clean too. She was the person anyone on the block could go to if they needed a place to stay. So I knew she would take me in.

Things got even sweeter when I got there because she told me she was leaving and I'd have the apartment to myself. She was moving to another town with her partner who had just gotten his place.

How much better could life get? Of course, not having my kids wasn't sweet and made life shitty. But this small win was a highlight during one of my lowest moments.

My aunt had three bedrooms and I had my own room. Thankful for a place to sleep comfortably, I excitedly headed to bed. I heard the bell ring—someone came looking for a place to sleep. My aunt called me out of my room to introduce me and I peeked around the corner. All I remember seeing was an afro and a man big as hell sitting on the couch. I said "Hello" and "Goodnight" all in the same breath.

In the days after she left for her partner's place, people she used to let rest there were knocking on the door all day and night—it was like the whole damn block needed a safe place. Geesh! I was overwhelmed, but still happy because I wasn't homeless. After a while, I had to tell people my aunt no longer lived there and that I wasn't comfortable just letting anyone in—especially because they were mostly men. I befriended a few of them and allowed them to rest their heads at times. 'Cause I know how hard it is to be homeless and without the safety of shelter. I was just grateful that after having everything stripped from me, I at least had a roof over my head.

Reader Reflection

There comes a moment when life pulls everything away—pride, comfort, even the masks we've learned to wear—and all that's left is the raw version of who we are. No filter. No armor. Just truth and survival.

This chapter was about being stripped down to your core—the kind of pain that forces you to rebuild from dust. It's not just about losing things or people; it's about facing yourself when there's nowhere left to hide.

When have you felt completely stripped of everything—and what did you discover about yourself in that moment?

_____

_____

_____

_____

_____

Think about the line: *It was just me, Sequoia, out in the world, fighting blindfolded. No direction. No guidance. Nothing.* What has it felt like for you to fight through life without a clear path— and what helped you find your way again?

_____

_____

_____

_____

_____

What kind of strength did you have to find when no one showed up for you?

_____

_____

_____

_____

_____

_____

If you could go back to a moment when you were scared, exhausted, and alone—what would you whisper to that version of you?

_____

_____

_____

_____

_____

_____

How did losing everything change your definition of "home"?

_____

_____

_____

_____

_____

Who do you want to become now that you've seen what surviving really costs?

_____

_____

_____

_____

_____

Remember: You were never broken—you were being rebuilt.

Chapter 10

Grimey Love

As I learned the area surrounding the Amsterdam Houses (my aunt's neighborhood), I'd walk to the store that was literally twelve blocks away. Most times it was for a cigarette. One day, on my way back up the hill, this tall, big-ass man chopped me right in my throat mid-pull on the cigarette—I damn near died.

"You don't remember me?", he asked.

I looked him up and down and said, "Hell no."

Then he explained that he was the guy from the night my aunt called me out of my room. As much as I wanted to fight him for that throat chop, I knew I would lose. He was too big and looked like a real crazy-ass man. I simply said, "Okay," (with attitude) and went on my way upstairs.

Later that night, I went outside with every intention of starting my shenanigans on this new block, but I ran into the Giant again. This time, he took me to get some food, then we sat outside talking. But this talk was different. We talked about life. We had so much in common in so many different ways. Then he said something that made me love him instantly: "I wanna meet your kids."

Even though he followed it up with his wild idea that I was gonna help him sell drugs—with walkie-talkies and me doing hand-to-hand—all I heard was that he wanted to meet my kids. He didn't care that I had just bared my soul and told him about the rapes, the arrest, and my kids being placed in foster care. He cared enough to know I needed support on those visits and offered to come with me next time.

Because he and I hit it off so well, he was one of the few men I let sleep in my aunt's house. Through him, I started getting to know some of the other people on the block. I don't know what people thought about me and the Giant, but I guess they assumed we were in a relationship because on one of his drunk nights, somebody brought him straight upstairs to my aunt's house and told me he was sleeping on the bench in the rain, drunk. I let him in and put his big ass on the couch where he slept.

Let me be clear, we weren't having sex, but we were using each other to get our shit off. After sobering up, he laid in bed with me and tried to rub my butt. What he didn't know was that I always slept with a switchblade tucked between my cheeks. So when he reached for me, he ran straight into my little cutter. Lol. Lucky for him, the switchblade was closed. I think he instantly thought I was crazy. But he also knew my story, because I had been vulnerable enough to tell him about my abuse.

I had never been to his mother's house or even met her, until the second "mistaken relationship" moment came. One day, she knocked on my aunt's door. I was shocked as hell—she didn't even say hello. She just said, "The Giant got locked up." Drugga had been to jail plenty of times, but the most I had ever done was write letters. But when she informed me about the Giant, I asked, "What do you need me to do?"

Please don't ask me why I said I'd go to court, but I did. And that was the day he officially became my boyfriend. We were locked in.

I would go with him to pick up his drugs and help him bag it. We'd make some money flipping it and then we'd go see my boys. It felt good being able to buy them whatever they wanted. After the visit, we'd hit the streets again and get right back to the money.

Life was good, though it would be better if my boys were home—you know how that goes. And my life being what it's always been, sent another curveball my way. My aunt returned home and I was homeless again after we had a big fight. So, I started staying at the Giant's grandmother's house. Not without drama, though. Every night, I had to wait in the hallway until he got his grandmother settled, then he'd sneak me in. I felt like I was in high school again—mind you, I was 20 years old.

One night, I had had enough. He left me in the house butt-ass naked and his grandmother came lurking around. She knew something was up and was determined to find me. I had to hide in his little-ass closet packed with clothes. I stayed so still, holding my breath while she poked around until he finally came back. I was annoyed as hell! After that incident, we decided to move into the trap house and that's where our relationship went to the next level. While he was out in the streets selling, I was in the house collecting—we weren't missing a dollar!

After a while—yup, you guessed it—I was pregnant. With all the stress, my body just wasn't ready, and I miscarried. Surprisingly, I wasn't sad, but he was. We got through it by making money—using that grind as our escape.

Eventually, his mother and I became cool. She was just happy her son had a girlfriend, I assume. The first time I witnessed her stealing from the Giant, I told him. But he already knew she'd been stealing his drugs for years, so I figured I would get my cut too. Lol. She'd steal some of his drugs to make her own money and I'd take extra from what he made for myself. We both minded our business until he started running out of money and drugs, and that's when he had enough and said if either one of us stole from him again it was going to be a problem. I immediately stopped, because the truth is I was stealing from myself since he'd give me the money anyway.

Our bond was like no other. We went everywhere together. And we did everything together. This was the love I wanted, the love I needed. All I needed now was my sons back home with me to feel complete. But God had other plans. I was pregnant again—and this child was here to stay. At 21, I was pregnant with my fourth son.

With me being pregnant, we decided that we needed a more suitable place, so we found a room through one of his friend's fathers. Ironically, it was on the same block where my mom had her room—just one house down. When I tell you I had a meltdown, it was crazy! Living on the same block my mother was killed on brought up so many emotions. While no charges were ever brought against her boyfriend at the time, nobody can tell me different—he was the cause behind my mother's death. Emotions aside, it seemed like something was bringing me back to her, or her back to me somehow. Strangely enough, I felt like it was a sign that she was by my side, protecting me.

At some point, I couldn't move around with the Giant anymore because I was far along in my pregnancy. I'd just stay in the room and he'd go out, make his money, and always come home in time for *The Simpsons*. After the show, we'd hit our favorite soul food spot, eat, and then return home to rest.

One day, he took me to the movies. As we were leaving, we ran into what felt like a thousand men on 125th Street. Somebody called out his name—"That's Grimey!"—and him being him, he started throwing up all his gang signs. My stomach was big as hell, so I tried to appeal to their morals. I unzipped my coat and said, "I'm pregnant. Please don't do this right now."

They didn't care. The first hit came right over my head. Somebody tried to smash him with a bottle, but he was ducking and dodging like a damn arcade game. We were literally fighting for our lives. Then somebody started shooting. I was standing right next to him—close enough that if the shooter wanted to, he could've blown my brains out.

But somehow, we made it out alive. We should have been scared. We should have felt our lives were in danger. Instead, we went home, laughed about it, and told the story to his friends.

After that incident, we bought a gun. I decided to lay low for the rest of my pregnancy, so he continued to hit his hood and make money while I stayed home. Somehow, he seemingly forgot he had a pregnant girlfriend. I knew he had a heavy addiction to dust at the time, so I was making excuses for him not coming home. He didn't show up for weeks at times. I was alone in that room, pregnant, with no money or food.

I decided to get up and go to the public assistance office down the block to get some emergency help. They gave me cash and food stamps that same day, and I used that to go down to his projects and see where he was. When I got off the train, someone must have made a phone call and told him they saw me. He came to the strip—that's what we called the block outside the projects—and met me. He took me to get food, and then we ended up relocating to another trap house in the back of the projects. I didn't notice at first that he unplugged the phone because I was present. I was just so happy to be eating and felt safe in his presence, that I didn't pay attention to the red flags.

The house we were staying at was his friend's mom's house, and the whole block was there because the mother had moved out. I kept telling the Giant I wanted to go buy food with the food stamps— there was a supermarket right behind the building—but he asked the time and said no, we had to wait. Another red flag I ignored.

One particular day, the owner of the apartment came to the house and we hit it off instantly. Her 17 year old daughter was there too and we clicked as well. While we were in the room talking, laughing, and getting to know each other, the phone rang. The daughter answered, and I guess the girl asked to speak to the Giant. Instead of the daughter telling him to come to the phone, she yelled for me to come get the call. The Giant ran behind me, and with my big-ass stomach, we were in there fighting over the phone.

The truth is, he was cheating on me the whole time, that's why he wasn't coming home. And the reason he never wanted to go to the supermarket was because the girl he was cheating with worked there. After the fight, he stormed out of the house and went to the strip. Then came the call, he was locked up. So close to my due date, too. I couldn't believe it, but it was real. Me and these damn storms.

It was such a devastating blow—I didn't know what to do. The woman (his friend's mother) whose apartment it was said, "Stay here with us until he comes home." And that's exactly what I did—I was blessed that they welcomed me with open arms. The daughter and I would go outside together and walk just to get some exercise in while I was going into my last stage of pregnancy. While outside one day, someone came up to me and said the girl the Giant was cheating on me with was looking for me. I was like, "You sure?" And once they confirmed it, I made sure she didn't have to look any further.

Now, I know what you're thinking: *You're pregnant.* And yes, I was— but I was still ready to fight whoever, whenever. Not that I didn't care about my unborn child, I just wasn't in the right headspace to fully comprehend that I could put my child in harm's way. Because I never just wanted to fight—I felt like if you were at a point where you wanna put your hands on me, I was gonna have to kill you. So me getting hit by someone was never a thought. I knew I was gonna beat the brakes off whoever I fought.

When that girl came outside after hours of me waiting for her, she acted like she didn't know she was looking for me. Lol. So I asked her real nice, "Do you wanna fight?" She said no. Maybe it was because I was pregnant, but either way, I was letting her know that if she did, I was available.

During the Giant's stay on Rikers, he would call the phone, and slowly we made up. I was always a sucker for love, and for some reason, I allowed men to mistreat me and then I'd go back. That was a bad habit I had. Once the Giant and I made up, I started making my way to visit him.

I don't know how long he was on Rikers, but I made every visit I could—pregnant and all. There were times I forgot my ID and had to go all the way back home, then come right back again. He never asked me to do those things, but because he had taken care of me, it only felt right that I took care of him.

While he was locked up, we lost the room that we were renting out. I couldn't make money being that pregnant, and he had lost all of his. So, I ended up back in the shelter system yet again. This time, it was harder—because I was pregnant and alone.

Reader Reflection

Sometimes love shows up wild—loud, protective, passionate—but underneath, it can carry control, chaos, or pain. When you've been through enough hurt, even broken love can feel like home, because it's familiar.

But this reflection is for you — the reader —the one who stayed when you knew it wasn't right, the one who mistook intensity for love, the one who gave all her softness to someone who didn't know how to hold it.

Think about a time you confused love with survival. How did it feel? What did it cost you?

_____

_____

_____

_____

_____

_____

_____

_____

_____

What parts of you have you silenced just to keep someone else comfortable?

_____

_____

_____

_____

_____

When was the last time you accepted less than you deserved because you didn't want to start over?

_____

_____

_____

_____

_____

Think about the line: *We went everywhere together. We did everything together. This was the love I wanted, the love I needed.* Have you ever wanted love so badly that you ignored how much it hurt you?

_____

_____

_____

_____

_____

_____

How would it feel to love yourself the way you keep trying to love someone else?

_____

_____

_____

_____

Remember: You deserve love that makes you feel safe and doesn't hurt you and/or rob you of your peace.

Chapter 11

The Bunker

T he Giant was finally released, but I didn't want to leave the shelter just yet. I stayed while he did what he needed to do to get his money back up. And in no time, I was giving birth. He made it to the hospital just in time to witness his first child being born. On July 25th, 2001, my fourth son came into the world.

Watching him be a father, loving on his child, was amazing. This was what I wanted for all my children. I never planned to have multiple fathers for my kids. I just wanted their fathers to love them and be present the way I was witnessing for the first time. He loved his son, in fact he loved all my children—that was a major plus.

But of course, you know this happy moment in my life couldn't come without pain. Being in the shelter alone with a newborn was so stressful. I wasn't getting any sleep, not because of the baby, but because of my living situation. I knew the Giant wasn't happy either. After brainstorming and trying to figure it out, we both realized we didn't want to continue house hopping and living with other people.

So, we came up with a plan to go into the shelter together. Since he was on my son's birth certificate, (another milestone I wasn't used to) we thought we could use that as leverage to get an apartment. I prepped him for the interview with the people from the shelter and told him everything to say. We practiced over and over again.

And as sure as shit, this man walked into that interview and said the complete opposite of everything we rehearsed. He told them he slept in Central Park and took baths in the bird pond. I tell you, it took everything in me not to punch him right there in that office! I'm sure the interviewer wanted to burst out laughing at this foolishness. When we left, I asked why he said the opposite of what we practiced. He told me that he had gotten nervous.

Somehow, they still gave us a ten-day placement. But on the tenth day, that dreaded letter slid under the door: ineligible. So now I had to come up with another plan. This time, I decided I'd go in alone with the baby and claim domestic violence. The story was that when we were found ineligible, he got mad and beat me up while the baby was in the room. That was our crazy plan and it worked.

Going back into the shelter system alone with a baby wasn't what I wanted, but it was what needed to be done if we were going to get our own place. I went to the EAU (Emergency Assistance Unit) once again and told them my story. They placed me in a ten-day placement. On the tenth day, I waited, praying no letter would come, and it didn't. I was so happy and knew we were going to be okay.

They placed us in Queens. The commute was hectic. I had to take the F train to the last stop, then walk a long distance to the shelter. It was a small hotel right off the highway, across from Jamaica Hospital and a few blocks from the Long Island Railroad (LIRR). I'd take the LIRR when visiting the Giant or coming back late because it was faster and easier.

While living in the shelter, there was this girl who always let her son play in the hallway. One day, her room filled up with smoke and the fire alarm went off. I ran in and started cursing her out. We got into a huge fight. Two days later, she showed up at my door with four garbage bags full of baby clothes, a peace offering. That week, my son was with his dad, so I invited her in to talk. We ended up sitting for hours talking, and somehow that conversation turned into us having sex. I don't know how or why, but it happened.

The next morning, I woke up and turned on the TV that was mounted on the wall. I thought I was watching an action movie. One plane crashed into a building, causing the building to crumble. Then I realized it was the news. The Twin Towers were under attack. It was surreal and devastating!

I started calling on the Lord asking for forgiveness. I thought the world was ending and I was being punished for having sex with that girl. As I snapped back to reality, I heard helicopters flying low over the hotel and army trucks rushing through the streets. It was like a movie and I was right in the middle of it. Then it hit me: I was alone. My children weren't with me and I needed to get to them.

I called the Giant and demanded he bring me my baby. He said no. I was furious and irrational. I didn't care that the trains weren't running. I tried to get to the Bronx to reach my other kids, but military officers turned me back. I was heartbroken because I couldn't reach my children. I wanted to make them feel safe, but I wasn't there and couldn't be there. I wanted to die.

Days passed. Slowly, the world started to stabilize. Phone lines were working again, so I called my children every chance I got. I met up with the Giant, got my son, and went to see my other kids. I didn't get to stay long because of the shelter curfew, but at least I saw them.

Weeks later, the world felt almost normal again and I was finally found eligible for Tier 2 placement. I was excited, until I got hit with a bomb. The agency called me in for a supervised visit with the other boys, and when I arrived with my baby, they told me the shelter had reported my "domestic violence" incident. Because I already had a case with Tee for domestic violence and assault, they took my baby right there on the spot.

The world went dark. I cried for weeks. During all my "planning", I never thought about how it could backfire. I'd heard women say domestic violence was the easiest way to get housing, so I thought I was being smart. But if I hadn't involved my newborn, maybe things would've been different. And just like that, another neglect case. Another loss.

Now I had to tell the Giant. When I called, he hung up on me. Once he processed it, we started trying to figure out where we wanted our son placed. My aunt already had my other kids, plus her own, so we tried his family. But none of them could take him.

My baby was placed with a foster mother. Despite everything, I believe things happen for a reason. On our first visit, the foster mother was kind and gave me space with my son. His dad didn't come, he was too emotional. I just stared at my baby, whispering apologies. I held back tears until the visit ended, then I broke down on the steps right in front of the ACS (Administration for Children) office.

My son's foster mother came out and asked if I was okay. She also wanted to know if I did drugs or had done something bad to my son. I told her no. Then she asked, "So why did they take your child?" I told her the truth. She looked at me and said, "Come to my house tomorrow and get your baby. The only time I need to see you is at the visits. Meet me a block away and we'll walk in like I had your child the whole time." And for a while, that's exactly what we did.

But just as that blessing came, the Giant got locked up again. Now I was back to navigating life alone, with another baby—no direction, no guidance, and no real help. I went back to live with the woman (his friend's mother) and her daughter, who I'd met when I found out the Giant was cheating. The mother moved out, leaving the apartment to me and her daughter. Things got wild when her brother came back to stay—we fought, stole from each other, and sold drugs. Eventually, me and the girl had a huge fight and she kicked me out.

I had nowhere to go. I sent my son back to the foster mother's house and slept on the trains for about a week. Hungry, dirty, and on my period, I finally built up the courage to go to the Giant's grandmother's house to ask his mom if I could shower and sleep. My body, mind, and heart were exhausted. She let me in and I slept like I hadn't in years. When I woke up, I learned that the Giant's mom had been arrested. I didn't know what to do, so I stayed at the grandmother's house until I made my next move.

Somehow, I reconnected with the young girl (Giant's friend's sister) and we squashed our beef. Eventually, we moved to the Bronx with her mom. It was around tax time and I had gotten a decent refund. Her brother owed someone money, so I gave him the cash to pay his debt. But he went and told his mother that I had money. When I came home that evening, I was confronted about the situation. They accused me of being sneaky and told me that I had to leave. Damn, no good deed goes unpunished.

Another week of sleeping on trains. Hungry, dirty, and worn down. Despite it all, I still visited my son at the foster agency and saw my other boys whenever I could. I was tired of crying. Tired of being homeless. Tired of this life.

My social worker was kind. He'd always ask about my plan, but I never had one. I was just tired. Tired of being homeless, tired of running from house to house, and tired of not having my children.

During one of our meetings, he confided that social work wasn't his passion. He planned to leave, but promised to stay until I got my kids back. Maybe he said it to motivate me, but it worked.

I told him the truth: I'd never get my kids back because I was homeless. I explained how I had my son daily, how the foster mother only came for visits, and how I was risking everything just to be with my baby. Then I came up with a plan. "If we just say I get my kids on weekends," I told him, "then I can go into the shelter system with them, and they'll give me housing big enough for all of us." He slid a computer in front of me and said, "Write the letter. Go get your sons and get back into the shelter." That was all I needed.

And for the first time in my life, a plan actually worked. I wrote the letter and he called my aunt to tell her I had permission to get my kids for the weekend. I picked up all four of my sons and went back into the shelter system one last time. On the tenth day, I waited by the door, silently praying that no paper would be slid under it. None came. Still, I gave it a few more days, just in case. Nothing. Finally, I exhaled. Thank God. My life began to turn around seemingly overnight.

Once I got the letter confirming permanent shelter placement, I took it to my social worker and we went back before the judge. On September 4th, 2003, my children were returned to me. We were placed in a Tier 2 shelter near the Highbridge section of the Bronx, right off the highway—for the first time, we were stable.

We started visiting their dad again. By then, we had decided to tell the kids that the Giant was their father, just to make them feel whole. He was already involved in their lives. What harm could a little "white lie" do? When the Giant came home, we were living in a big three-bedroom apartment in Hunts Point. Our family was back together and felt complete.

Once we were stable, I kept my promise to my mother. I spoke with my aunt and she agreed to let my sister and brother come live with me. My little cousin and her boyfriend came around too, and so did my aunt's kids. My house was always full of kids and I loved it.

We were happy. Life was amazing. But because it's me, it didn't take long for the storm to locate me as usual. The only difference now? I was wiser. Stronger. Ready for whatever storm came my way. Because **I am the bunker.**

I survived things that were meant to destroy me—sexual abuse, childhood trauma, abandonment, homelessness, the system, toxic relationships, the streets, and loss. I lost my anchors (my mother and my Grandmother) and momentarily lost my children and myself—yet I still somehow found the strength to rise again. I am here because I always rose—wiser, stronger, and rooted in something no storm could wash away.

There were chapters of my life that read like tragedy stacked on top of tragedy, like God was testing how much one heart could hold. But even when I was stripped of everything—a roof over my head, security, dignity, and peace—by the grace of God, I was never truly uprooted. Every storm was shaping me, preparing me for who I was becoming.

Like the sequoia trees that grow taller than almost anything on this earth, I learned that survival wasn't my final form—growth was. Sequoias don't just survive fire, they **need** it. The flames crack open the seed. The same way pain cracked me open and woke up a strength I didn't know lived inside me. And like my namesake, the Cherokee leader Sequoyah—who carved language for his people—I found my voice after years of silence. I turned pain into my story/testimony, survival into legacy, and truth into power.

This is not a fairy tale ending. It's not even where the story ends. This is a **woman standing in her becoming. I am Sequoia—I am rooted and I am rising.** And I want you to know that you too can come back from anything. Some of us weren't meant to burn down—we were made to rise through the ashes tall as hell.

Reader Reflection

You learned what it felt like to fight for your family and for stability. You had to make a plan not knowing what the outcome would be.

This page is for you: the person who's done whatever it took for their loved ones, made a plan when none existed, and held it together when it felt impossible.

Use this space to reflect on the ways you survived, the compromises you made, and the truths that shaped the next version of yourself. Write slow and breathe between lines.

When have you made a risky plan to protect someone you love?

_____

_____

_____

_____

_____

_____

_____

What did "home" feel like to you when you finally got it, even if it was fragile or temporary?

_____

_____

_____

_____

_____

_____

Who helped you when the world closed in—a social worker, a neighbor, a stranger—and how did that help change the outcome?

_____

_____

_____

_____

_____

_____

Think about the line: *I am the bunker.* What does being the bunker mean to you—protection, stubbornness, safety, or something else?

_____

_____

_____

_____

_____

What did you learn about asking for help versus doing it all yourself?

_____

_____

_____

_____

_____

If you could give one practical piece of advice to someone trying to keep their family together, what would it be?

_____

_____

_____

_____

_____

_____

_____

_____

_____

_____

_____

_____

Remember: You did what you needed to do. Give yourself grace. What may have broken others strengthened you— you are the bunker.

Meet the Author

Sequoia Patterson is a mother of five, community activist, and Hospital Responder Supervisor committed to breaking cycles of violence and generational pain. A survivor of abuse, homelessness, and the justice system, she channels her lived experiences into healing and hope for others.

Her first publication in the bestselling anthology, *If These Scars Could Talk*, introduced readers to her powerful story of survival. Now, she expands upon that truth in this full-length memoir—unflinching, unapologetic, and deeply human. Through her words and her work, Sequoia proves that even in darkness, transformation is possible.